# SELF DISCOVERY JOURNAL FOR BALANCE AND HARMONY

*Reflections on all the parts of you*

MICHELLE FRALEY

This book is dedicated to my greatest sources
of love and light, Nick and Sierra

# GUIDED JOURNAL FOR SELF-DISCOVERY AND BALANCE

*Reflections on all the parts of YOU Michelle Fraley, MA, WPCC*

**INTRODUCTION**: Welcome friends. I am so glad you are here. Whether you are a seasoned journaler or new to journaling, this book is designed to facilitate a deeper understanding of your thoughts and feelings. Each section of this journal will offer you thoughtful and exciting prompts to create awareness and clarity so that you can become your own best source of wisdom and guidance. Through this practice of prompted journaling, your spirit and soul will be given an opportunity to express itself through the lens of compassion and truth. This profound knowledge will allow you to navigate your life in ways that lead to fulfillment, joy and abundance. This journal will create space for you to listen, observe and learn about yourself. This practice of personal reflection will allow you to become your own internal compass and rely less on the opinions of others.

Keep in mind that journaling may uncover thoughts, feelings and memories that are difficult or uncomfortable. Journaling is always done with a sense of curiosity and compassion, never shame or guilt. When we approach self-discovery in a kind and gentle manner, we are more likely to use the data we have collected to improve our lives and grow, rather than shame ourselves into regression or stagnation. What do you do if you struggle with this process or use a shaming voice? I invite you to give yourself some grace, seek support from a source of loving kindness or perhaps even take a break, step away for a time, and return to journaling when you feel more regulated. There is no need to hurry, rush or force this process. Learning to take care of yourself is part of the growth.

**WHY JOURNALING?** We are more motivated to stick with a new habit when we have a deeper sense of why the habit is beneficial to our well-being. These are just a few benefits that a regular and consistent journaling practice can provide.

1. Journaling is a great way to have a conversation with yourself and check in with your thoughts and feelings. Every time you journal, you are sending your brain a signal that you matter and that your thoughts and feelings are worthy of being heard.

2. Journaling can help you tap into your core values and become aware of what truly matters to you. This is important knowledge for creating authentic life balance.

3. Journaling can help you create tangible action plans. When your thoughts have structure and organization, it may feel easier to determine the next steps.

4. Journaling can hold space for thoughts and feelings that are not yet clear. This process can allow you to express snippets of what is on your mind and then return later to create deeper clarity.

5. Journaling gives you an opportunity to practice self-compassion and self-love.

6. Lastly, journaling can help improve mood, self-soothe and promote personal growth. Writing positive thoughts can increase our happiness hormones (serotonin and dopamine), while writing about distressing and difficult feelings can lead to lower levels of the stress hormone, cortisol. Simply put, journaling can be an easy, inexpensive and effective way to regulate our nervous system and manage stress.

**TIPS FOR JOURNALING:** Full disclosure – I had an on-again/off-again relationship with journaling for much of my life. I would start and stop the practice over and over again. I just couldn't seem to stick with it, no matter how much I wanted to. I can now say that I have been in a committed relationship with my journaling practice for over a decade. This practice has been instrumental in helping me self-reflect, self-soothe, identify my triggers, heal my wounds, achieve my goals, regulate my stress, create balance in my life and simply spend time with myself in a kind and compassionate way. Here are a few of my favorite tips for starting and maintaining a consistent journaling practice.

1. Let go of the idea that "consistent" must mean daily! You do not have to journal daily to journal consistently. Set a flexible schedule that works for you and allow yourself to flow with the practice, pivoting and changing your schedule as needed. Your journaling practice may ebb and flow with the seasons in your life and that is ok.

2. Make journaling a habit by being consistent about the time and place of your journaling. You don't have to be rigid with your routine, but having a consistent ritual around time and place can help make journaling a habit you'll stick with.

3. Recognize that you are worthy of being heard in all your many moods and seasons of life, not just when you are stressed or in crisis. We can unintentionally create a negative association with journaling if we only journal when life feels hard, so I recommend journaling during all stages of your life journey.

4. Let go of expectations of how your journaling "should look." How much and what you write is your choice. Your journaling can be a few words or a few pages. Also, keep in mind that your journaling experience is not being critiqued or graded, so just be honest and have fun with the process. Do your best not to overthink your grammar, handwriting and spelling.

5. Journal in a place with limited distractions. Avoid multitasking and put your phone away. No checking email or Instagram while you journal. You deserve your full attention.

6. Journaling does not need to be a linear process. If you need to skip a prompt (or even a full section) and return to it later, no problem! Feel free to jump around this book in whatever way feels best to you. This is YOUR journey!

# The many parts of you:

# CHAPTER 1:
# THE EARLY YEARS

There is no denying that our early childhood experiences help to shape who we are now. Creating awareness around these experiences can help us understand our thoughts, feelings, behaviors and triggers. Examining our past is never done under the umbrella of shame or regret, but rather with a sense of compassion and curiosity. I invite you to explore these prompts about your childhood in a playful, gentle and kind manner.

1. What three words best describe your childhood?

2. Finish this sentence: As a child, I could spend hours....

3. Finish this sentence: As a child, I worried about...

4. What do you remember most about your mom when you were a child?

5. What do you remember most about your dad when you were a child?

6. What do you remember most about your siblings when you were a child?

7. Describe one of your earliest childhood memories that still makes you feel happy?

8. What made you mad when you were a child?

9.  What smells remind you of your childhood?

10. What were some of your favorite meals growing up?

11. What traditions did you have in your family when you were a child?

12.  Describe a childhood friend and what that friend meant to you.

13.  What expectations were put on you as a child?

14.  What natural talents did you display as a child?

15. What were you praised for as a child?

16. When you were a child, what did you want to do when you grew up?

17. What music did you listen to as a child? Did you have a favorite musical artist or group?

18. What was the best thing about your childhood?

19. What makes your childhood unique?

20. What would surprise your childhood self about you now?

# CHAPTER 2: FAMILY

The word "family" can mean different things to different people. Some of us define family as our nuclear family, while others may include their extended family or "chosen" family. No matter how you define family, understanding your family dynamics and family systems can be instrumental in learning about yourself. Use the following prompts to explore your own connection to family.

1.  What three words best describe your family?

2.  What do you believe to be true about your family?

3.   What does your family collectively value?

4.   What does your family struggle with?

5.   What is unique or different about your family?

6.  How does your family show love?

7.  Is your family physically affectionate? Discuss.

8.  How does your family have fun together?

9.  What is/was your relationship like with your grandparents?

10. Is the idea of legacy important to your family?

11. What worries you about your family?

12. Does your family have a history of any unhealthy patterns? Discuss.

13. What fascinates you about other peoples' families?

14. What lessons have you learned from being a part of your family?

15. What lessons have you taught your family?

16. Is there anything you would like to say to your family? If so, say it here.

17. What family traditions have you carried on or created within your family?

18. Have you had pets in your family? If so, take a moment to remember them here.

19. Describe a memorable travel experience with your family.

20. How does your family typically celebrate birthdays and holidays?

# CHAPTER 3:
# SELF-DISCOVERY

Self-discovery is what happens when we are curious about ourselves. When we have a growth mindset and take the time to show interest in our thoughts, feelings, desires and goals. Self-discovery can be deeply reflective or whimsical and lighthearted. When we create space to know who we are, we can show up as our most authentic selves. Cultivating awareness about ourselves in our current season of life allows us to lean into the best version of who we can be. Answer these prompts mindfully and in the present tense. This section isn't about who you were; it is about who you are.

1.   What five words best describe who you are today?

2.   What are 10 things that just feel like a "yes" in your life right now?

3.  What are five foods that you always have on hand?

4.  If you were a color, what color would you be and why?

5.  How do you make the world a better place or contribute to society?

6. What five songs could you listen to on repeat?

7. How would you describe your style?

8. Do you consider yourself creative? Why or why not?

9.   What have you been avoiding lately?

10.  When are you most at ease?

11.  When was the last time you cried, and why?

12. What possessions do you own that are precious to you?

13. What is a recent purchase you made that you feel good about?

14. Do you consider yourself adventurous? Why or why not?

15. Finish this prompt: Some of my favorite things to do are…

16. What do you wish you had more of in your life right now?

17. What do you wish you had less of in your life right now?

18. What is something you could teach others?

19. What frustrates you the most about your daily life?

20. Describe your "happy place."

# CHAPTER 4: SELF-TALK AND NARRATIVES

The way we speak to ourselves matters. Our inner dialogue influences our feelings and behaviors and creates our reality. We tend to be more mindful of how we use our words with others than how we speak to ourselves. We often believe what we think, so our inner voice must reflect the person we want to be. I invite you to take some time to examine your self-talk with these prompts.

1.  Do you have any beliefs about yourself that hold you back from happiness?

2.  What do you believe about yourself that feels true and authentic?

3.  What is the best way for you to motivate yourself?

4.  Do you consider yourself to be an overthinker? Why or why not?

5.  What has been consuming your thoughts lately?

6.  What would you like to think less about?

7.  Do you tend to procrastinate? Discuss.

8.  Describe your inner critic. What does it look like or sound like?

9. What is a quote or saying that inspires you?

10. What is the kindest thing you could say to yourself when you are suffering or in pain?

11. What makes compassionate self-talk difficult for you?

12. How would your life be different if you had less negative self-talk?

13. Is there a belief you need to release and let go of to move forward?

14. Are you a good friend to yourself? Why or why not?

15. If you could choose to fully believe one thing about yourself, what would it be?

16. Do you struggle to stay in the present moment? Discuss?

17. Do you believe that you can choose your thoughts? Why or why not?

18. If you could choose anyone to be the voice of your inner dialogue, who would you choose and why?

19. Do you enjoy spending time with your own thoughts? Why or why not?

20. What is the general quality of your daily thoughts? Do they tend to be positive or negative?

28

# CHAPTER 5: VALUES AND PRIORITIES

Knowing our values and guiding principles is essential to living a happy, healthy, balanced life. Knowing our priorities is the first step in designing an ideal life. To invest our time in the right people, places and experiences, we must know what matters most to us. Once we create this awareness, we can be proactive in designing a life that aligns with our values. It has been said that if we don't know what truly matters to us, there is a good chance that someone else (parents, peers, social media) will tell us. Use the following prompts to gain insight into what really matters to you.

1. Map out your ideal day from waking until bedtime..

2. What do you wish you had more time to do?

3. What does your gut tell you that you were made to do?

4. What are you most proud of in your life and why?

5. Describe three people that you admire.

6. What do you spend time on that doesn't really matter to you?

7. If you didn't fear the judgment of others, what would you do more of?

8. What do you want to be remembered for?

9.   What do you often talk about doing, but never actually do?

10.  Beyond your basic human needs, what must you have in your life to experience true happiness and fulfillment?

11.  Finish this sentence: I want to focus more on....

12. If you wrote a book, what would you write about?

13. If you could travel anywhere in the world, where would you go and why?

14. If you could have a conversation with anyone, past or present, who would it be and why?

15. What do you feel passionate about protecting?

16. What is something you've always wanted to do, but never done?

17. What can you honestly say you've worked hard at this year?

18. Finish this sentence: I am truly inspired by…

19. What really matters to you now that didn't matter as much to you 10 years ago?

20. In what ways do you want to grow and improve?

# CHAPTER 6: LIFE BALANCE

Once we know what matters most to us, we are in a much better position to begin creating balance in our lives. Awareness of our values allows us to focus on what brings us happiness and fulfillment. Authentic alignment is the key to life balance. If we aren't aware of what we value, we are likely spending our time and energy in the wrong places. Allow these journaling prompts to ignite your intuition and guide you toward a state of authentic alignment and true life balance.

1.   Finish this sentence: In my life right now, I have too much…

2.   Finish this sentence: In my life right now, I have too little…

3.   Finish this sentence: In my life right now, I feel balanced in...

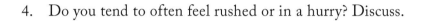

4.   Do you tend to often feel rushed or in a hurry? Discuss.

5.   Who or what really deserves your time, energy and attention right now?

6. Describe a time in your life when you felt your most balanced. What was different about that time versus now?

7. How are you over-functioning or taking responsibility for others?

8. Is there anything missing in your life right now?

9. How do you seek or create peace?

10. What types of environments help you feel balanced and at ease?

11. What kinds of environments pull you out of balance?

12. Is there anything you are forcing in your life right now that just isn't working for you?

13. What do you need to say no to to create more balance in your life?

14. What do you spend time and energy doing that feels like a waste?

15. If you had two extra hours each day, how would you like to spend them?

16. How has the concept of life balance changed for you over time?

17. Describe someone you know who is a good role model for life balance.

18. How does technology and the digital world affect your life balance?

19. What could you reasonably commit to doing this month to restore balance in your life?

20. Finish this sentence: I know I am in balance when....

# CHAPTER 7: CONFIDENCE

Once we understand what we need to create life balance, confidence is what allows us to take action. When we are moving through life with confidence, we know that we are enough and have nothing to prove. Confidence reminds us that we have every right to follow our dreams and show up for our unique journey. Some benefits of boosting your confidence include less fear of rejection, increased assertiveness and willingness to speak your truth, decreased negative self-talk and a boost in emotional resilience. Use the following prompts to reflect on your relationship with confidence.

1. Finish this sentence: I feel best about myself when…

2. What are three of your biggest strengths?

3. Discuss two ways you've grown or improved over the past year.

4. What advice would you give your younger self about confidence?

5. In what areas of your life do you feel the most confident?

6. What compliments do you regularly receive?

7. In what areas do you tend to compare yourself to others?

8. How would your life be different if you had more confidence?

9. Finish this sentence: The thing about myself that makes me the proudest is…

10. What are two things that you consider yourself to be an "expert" in?

11. Do you have any hidden talents? If so, explain.

12. What is something you just know you're amazing at?

13. What would you say no to if you had more confidence?

14. What are you truly working on improving in your life right now?

15. Describe a time in life when you failed and how that experience helped you grow.

16. What is something you accomplished that seemed impossible at the time.

17. Do you hesitate or have trouble making decisions? Discuss.

18. Would you describe yourself as a complainer? If so, what do you regularly complain about?

19. How do you think confidence differs from arrogance?

20. What do you need to let go of to feel fully confident?

# CHAPTER 8: HEALTH AND WELLNESS

It is no secret that our health, both physical and emotional, influences how we experience every other area of our lives. If we are struggling or in pain, it is very difficult to show up as our most balanced, authentic and aligned selves. Suffering in any form can push us into a sympathetic nervous system state of fight, flight or freeze resulting in stress and reactivity. Use the following prompts to gain insight into your current state of health and wellness and use the data you collect to create a healthier and happier you.

1.  Does your body allow you to participate in your life as you would like? Why or why not?

2. Do you have any chronic pain issues? If yes, describe what's going on.

3. Do you take time for preventative health care? Why or why not?

4. List five ways you take good care of your body.

5.  Describe any serious injuries or illnesses you've had. Did you fully recover?

6.  Have you ever felt disappointed in your body's ability to heal?

7.  How do you tend to treat your body when you are sick or injured?

8. Is there anything your body needs right now that you are not giving it?

9. Do you often find yourself worrying about your physical health? Discuss.

10. Describe your relationship with sleep?

11. What small change could you make today to improve your physical health?

12. Who inspires you to live a healthy lifestyle?

13. What emotions and feelings have been showing up for you recently?

14. List three ways that you take care of your emotional health.

15. What emotions do you tend to have difficulty expressing?

16. Do you give yourself permission to cry? Why or why not?

17. Are you more likely to worry about the past or the future? Discuss.

18. Do you generally feel like your mind is a source of comfort or stress? Discuss.

19. What is something you could do today to positively impact your emotional health?

20. Finish this sentence: I want to feel more...

# CHAPTER 9: CAREER

Whether you work full-time, part-time or not at all, thinking about what career and business mean to you can be enlightening. Everyone places a differing value on career and work. For some people, a career is an extension of their values and life purpose. Others may use a career as simply a means to an end and find purpose elsewhere. Use these prompts to better understand your relationship with career and business.

1.  Describe your feelings about your current job or career.

2.  How did you get into this line of work?

3. What training or education prepared you for this career? And did you feel prepared?

4. Does your job align with your natural skills and abilities? Discuss.

5. Does your job include duties that feel out of your comfort zone? Discuss?

6. Are you satisfied with your compensation, financial or otherwise, at your current job?

7. What keeps you working at your current job?

8. Discuss a past job that you had that made an impact on your life.

9. Do you think your current job will be your last job? Why or why not?

10. What are three things you enjoy about your job?

11. What are three things you would like to change about your job?

12. What memorable relationships have you created at work?

13. What job or career have you never tried but think you'd be good at?

14. What job or career would just be a total "NO" for you? Why?

15. How do you feel at the beginning of a workday?

16. How do you feel at the end of a workday?

17. Would you encourage others to go into your line of work? Why or why not?

18.  How does your job affect other areas of your life?

19.  What life lessons have you learned from your job or career?

20.  If you didn't have to work, would you? Why or why not?

# CHAPTER 10: GRATITUDE

Experts in the field of positive psychology tell us that gratitude is highly correlated with happiness and overall life satisfaction. Current research in neuropsychology further suggests that the greatest benefits of gratitude arise when we actively express gratitude rather than passively "having" gratitude. Use the following prompts to express gratitude for your unique and beautiful life.

1. Write a list of 20 things you are grateful for?

2. What does gratitude mean to you?

3. How do you tend to express gratitude?

4. What three things do you appreciate most about your life right now?

5. Write a short thank you note to someone who has positively impacted your life.

6. What was the best thing you learned from your mother?

7. What was the best thing you learned from your father?

8. What is a skill you have that you are grateful for?

9.   What is a life lesson that you are grateful for learning?

10.  What is a hobby you have that you are grateful for?

11.  What are three things you are grateful for about where you live?

12. What simple pleasure in your everyday life are you grateful for?

13. What is something you are grateful for today that you previously took for granted?

14. What tastes are you most grateful for?

15. What smells are you most grateful for?

16. What sounds are you most grateful for?

17. What makes gratitude difficult for you to express?

18. Who deserves credit for the good in your life?

19. What types of celebrations or ceremonies make you feel grateful?

20. Are you satisfied with your relationship with gratitude? Why or why not?

# CHAPTER 11: SELF-LOVE

Self-love is a misunderstood concept. Many confuse it with arrogance, when, in fact, self-love is about showing up for yourself with the same kindness, curiosity, compassion and grace that you do for others. Practicing self-love creates an atmosphere of worthiness and abundance so that you can love both yourself and others in a healthy and authentic way. Loving yourself also teaches others how to love you. Use these prompts to help foster and cultivate more self-love in your own life.

1.  Write a list of 10 things that feel good to your heart.

2.  What three things do you appreciate most about yourself?

3.  What are five things you can do to nurture yourself when you're feeling down?

4.  How do you celebrate your accomplishments?

5.  What is one thing you need to come to peace with and why?

6. Finish this sentence: I show myself love by...

7. What gets in the way of showing yourself love?

8. Do you give yourself permission to seek pleasure in all its forms? Discuss

9. How does social media impact your self-love?

10. Who in your life is a good example of self-love?

11. What have you created that you are proud of?

12. Do you consider yourself to be a perfectionist? Why or why not?

13. What part of yourself would you like to learn more about?

14. What qualities of yourself do you love to share with others?

15. What is the best compliment you could give yourself?

16. Finish this sentence: If I truly loved myself, I would....

17. Describe a recent act of self-love.

18. What is one thing you could realistically add to your everyday life to show yourself more love?

19. What do you need to release to fully embrace self-love?

20. Write the words you need to hear today to feel loved.

# CHAPTER 12: FEAR

Fear is something many of us avoid because we distortedly believe that thinking about fear will make us feel more anxious when, in fact, trying to distract ourselves from fear actually causes more suffering. Deep down, we know that knowledge is power. When we face our fears head-on and gain clarity around what is making us feel uneasy and uncomfortable, we can show up for ourselves and manage our fear in healthy and effective ways. It is normal for humans to feel fear; it keeps us safe, but it can also keep us stuck. Use these prompts to create awareness around fear and how it appears in your life.

1. What are you afraid of?

2. What is causing tension in your life right now?

3.   What is a thought that has been getting the best of you lately?

4.   How do you distract yourself from uncomfortable feelings?

5.   Do you experience fear in social situations? Discuss.

6. What fear is in the way of you reaching your goals?

7. Describe a time when you have pushed past your fear. What happened?

8. What is something that used to scare you but no longer causes fear?

9. What types of situations bring out your most fearful self?

10. Describe how it feels to disagree with others or share your opinions when they differ from others.

11. Finish this sentence: I would like to stop being afraid of...

12. What parts of you are you scared to share with others?

13. In what ways has fear been helpful to you?

14. What life lessons have you learned from fear?

15.  Are you scared of success? Why or why not?

16.  How do you project your fears onto others?

17.  Who do you consider to be fearless and why?

18. What is your relationship like with change and uncertainty?

19. When making a decision, do you seek a lot of outside opinions before moving forward?

20. Courage is defined as acting even when you're afraid. When was the last time you did something courageous?

# CHAPTER 13: BOUNDARIES

Boundaries are guidelines about what is acceptable and unacceptable in our relationships. Contrary to popular belief, boundaries are not mean, nor are they meant to control others. Instead, boundaries allow you to clearly express your needs and expectations and are essential in healthy relationships. Relationships thrive on transparency and open communication. Boundaries allow us to stop hinting at our needs and instead allow us to clearly and authentically communicate. Use these prompts to create awareness around your own boundaries and how you may want to integrate them into your relationships.

1.  What physical boundaries do you prefer to have with others? (physical touch, personal space)

2.  What emotional boundaries do you prefer to have with others? (vulnerability, sharing)

3.  What type of material boundaries do you prefer to have with others? (lending or borrowing personal effects)

4.  What type of time-oriented boundaries do you prefer to have with others? (time spent socializing, working)

5.  If you were being completely honest with yourself, what boundaries do you need to create in your life right now?

6. Is there anything or anyone in particular you struggle to set boundaries with? Why is this so difficult for you?

7. Would you consider yourself a people pleaser? Why or why not?

8. What do you need to protect in your life right now?

9. How do you tend to manage conflict?

10. How do you react when you think someone is upset or disappointed with you?

11. What did you learn about boundaries from your family?

12. How would your life be different if you had healthy boundaries with others?

13. Do you tend to take responsibility for things that aren't yours to own?

14. How does it feel to ask for help?

15. How does it feel to say no when someone has a request or asks you for a favor?

16. How do you feel when someone sets a boundary with you?

17. In what areas of your life are you comfortable setting boundaries?

18. What boundaries do you want to create with yourself?

19. Who in your life is a healthy role model for boundaries?

20. Finish this sentence: I am worthy of...

# CHAPTER 14: LIFE TRANSITIONS

Change, growth and evolution are natural parts of the human experience. We often resist change because change brings uncertainty, and uncertainty makes us feel uncomfortable. Lucky for us humans, our brains are flexible and designed to learn and evolve. Acknowledging the changes in our lives allows us to effectively manage change and use it for healthy growth. I invite you to explore the following prompts to examine your own life transitions and your relationship with change.

1.  What life transitions are you currently experiencing?

2.  What are you welcoming into your life with these changes?

3.  What are you saying goodbye to with these changes?

4.  What life transitions are you looking forward to?

5.  Do you consider yourself to be a changemaker? Why or why not?

6.  How are you currently resisting change in your life?

7.  What role has grief played in your life?

8.  What helps make the process of change easier and more comfortable for you?

9. Who can you rely on for support during times of change and uncertainty?

10. Are you likely to ask for help during challenging times? Why or why not?

11. What life lessons have you learned from past seasons of change?

12. What advice would you give to your younger self about managing change?

13. What life transitions could you help guide others through?

14. What is your favorite season of the year and why?

15. How do you like to celebrate your birthday?

16. How do you like to celebrate the new year? Do you make resolutions? Why or why not?

17. Who in your life do you consider to be a "change warrior" – someone who easily handles change?

18. What life change are you committed to making in the next year?

19. Describe a life change that was bittersweet.

20. What do you consider to be your most life-changing experience to date?

# CHAPTER 15: BODY IMAGE

Creating a healthy dynamic between our mind, body and spirit is essential for living a holistically balanced life. If there is tension and toxicity with our body we may struggle with self-trust, intimacy and confidence. The way we talk to our body influences our thoughts and feelings about our body and even how our body functions. Use the following prompts to create awareness around your relationship with your body.

1. What one word best describes your current relationship with your body?

2. What one word best describes your ideal relationship with your body?

3. What part of your body gives you the most pride?

4. What part of your body do you struggle to accept?

5. Which of your five senses is the strongest?

6.  When do you feel most at ease in your body?

7.  What is your body longing for right now?

8.  How have your thoughts about your body changed over time?

9. If your body could talk to you, what would it say?

10. What do you think your body needs more of right now?

11. What do you think your body needs less of right now?

12. What question would you like to ask your body?

13. What are some of your favorite ways to move your body?

14. Describe your relationship with sleep? Are you satisfied with the amount and quality of your sleep? Why or why not?

15. Describe your relationship with caffeine?

16. Describe your relationship with alcohol?

17. What is the coolest thing your body ever did?

18. Finish this sentence: My body is worthy of…

19. What is one small change you could make today to honor your body?

20. Write a short thank you note to your body.

# CHAPTER 16: GOALS AND DREAMS

According to famous psychiatrist and author, Viktor Frankl, purpose keeps us motivated to live. Without purpose, we are just going through the motions…surviving without really living. Awareness of our goals and dreams allows us to create strategies to work towards them in realistic and attainable ways. Larger life goals can be broken down into smaller, everyday actions. Even "out there" dreams or goals that feel unattainable can keep us motivated and enthusiastic about life. We can find happiness in practicality and in reaching for the stars. Explore the following prompts to gain insight into your own unique goals and dreams.

1.   Finish this sentence: I wish…

2.  What is something you regularly daydream about?

3.  What is something you want to do, but feel like it's too big to tackle?

4.  What goals and dreams do other people have for you?

5.  What is something that you often talk about doing, but never actually do?

6.  What have you seen others accomplish that inspires you?

7.  If you woke up tomorrow and your life was suddenly perfect, what would be different?

8. Imagine yourself one year from now...what goal will you have accomplished?

9. Who are the biggest supporters of your goals and dreams?

10. What gets in the way of you achieving your goals and dreams?

11. What dreams have you let die and why?

12. What dreams of yours have become reality?

13. Do you have a bucket list? If so, what's on it?

14. Have you ever thought you wanted something and then, when you got it, realized you didn't actually want it?

15. What is the scariest dream you have ever chased?

16. What scares you more, failure or regret? Discuss.

17. What inner strengths do you possess that could make reaching your goals and dreams more likely?

18. If you could have one superpower, what would it be?

19. If you could have anyone (dead or alive) as a mentor for your goals and dreams, who would it be?

20. What is a goal or dream you refuse to give up on?

# CHAPTER 17: STRESS AND WORRY

Stress and worry are both big contributors to stagnation in our personal growth. Stress and worry keep us stuck in unhealthy patterns. They also give us a host of uncomfortable physical and emotional symptoms. Stress (which comes from the body) can look like body aches, joint pain, inflammation, fatigue, headaches, sleep disturbances, sexual dysfunction and digestive issues. Worry (which comes from the brain) can look like overthinking, catastrophizing, taking things too personally and ruminating. Creating awareness around our stress and worry can help us manage our symptoms, mitigate our triggers and strengthen our overall emotional resilience. Use the following prompts to reflect on your own relationship with stress and worry.

1.  How does stress show up in your body?

2. When you feel stress, are you more likely to fight, flight or freeze? Discuss.

3. How do you currently manage your physical stress? How effective are these techniques?

4. What have you thought about trying for stress management, but haven't actually done?

5. What triggers can you identify that create stress in your body?

6. Do you like activities that activate your stress response, such as roller coasters or jump-scare movies?

7. Do you engage in any strategies to manage stress that you consider to be unhealthy?

8. What do you tend to worry about most often?

9. What are you worried about right now?

10. Do you worry more about the past or the future?

11. Do your worries show up in your dreams?

12. Do you consider yourself an optimist or a pessimist? How does this contribute to worry?

13. What triggers can you identify that cause you to worry?

14. What helps ease your worry?

15. How would your life be different if you didn't invest so much time into worrying?

16. Who do you use as a source of support when you are stressed or worried?

17. Have you ever worked with a coach or therapist? If so, was it helpful?

18. Do people often come to you for support and advice when they are stressed or worried?

19. How do your stress and worry impact your daily life?

20. How do your stress and worry impact the lives of others?

# CHAPTER 18:
# COMMUNICATION

How we communicate with others is how we express our energy, emotions, needs, desires, frustrations, disappointments and hurts. Communication is broad and includes honesty, vulnerability, intention, clarity, conflict resolution, listening skills, tone of voice and body language. There is a lot of truth in the phrase, "It isn't always what you say, but how you say it." The way we communicate defines our dynamics with others. Use these prompts to create an understanding of your own communication style and tendencies.

1. Do you believe that what you have to say matters? Why or why not?

2. Do you consider yourself an introvert or an extrovert?

3. Do you consider yourself a good communicator? Why or why not?

4. How do you think others would describe your communication style?

5. How do you tend to manage conflict in relationships?

6. Do you agree or disagree with this statement: "Don't ever go to bed mad."

7. How does it feel to voice your opinion if it is different from others?

8. How likely are you to ask for help? Discuss.

9. What holds you back from speaking your truth or sharing your opinion?

10. Who truly knows the "real" you? Who do you take the mask off in front of?

11. What does your body language tell others about you?

12. What do you wish others knew about you?

13. What do you wish you had the courage to say out loud?

14. Do you consider yourself a "gossip".

15. Who in your life has taught you a valuable lesson about communication?

16. How could you become a better communicator?

17. Who in your life could be considered a communication role model?

18. Do you enjoy being the center of attention? Why or why not?

19. What topics are difficult for you to discuss?

20. What topics do you enjoy talking about?

# CHAPTER 19: FRIENDSHIP

Research in positive psychology tells us one of the most significant factors correlated with happiness is the quality of our social connections. As humans, we are built for connection and thrive when we feel accepted and part of a community. In our full lives, we often let our social relationships whither under the excuse of being "too busy" and subsequently feel lonely and disconnected. Many of us also find socializing or making new friends difficult and, hence, feel isolated and alone. Use these prompts to explore your friendships and social life.

1. Describe the three most significant friendships in your life right now.

2. Who are some of your other favorite people to spend time with?

3. Do you have a best friend?

4. Is the idea of a best friend important to you?

5. What is a life lesson you have learned from friendship?

6. How have your friendships changed over the years?

7. Do you prefer one-on-one socializing or groups? Discuss.

8. Describe the ideal friend you'd like to manifest.

9. What makes a friend different from an acquaintance?

10. What types of things do you like to do with your friends?

11. Who in your life would you like to spend more time with? Why aren't you spending more time with them?

12. Which of your friends knows the "real" you?

13. Are you satisfied with how you are showing up for your friends?

14. What would your friends say they love most about you?

15. What friendships in your life have withstood the test of time?

16. Do you have any frenemies?

17. Describe a friendship that disappointed you.

18. Have you ever experienced a friendship breakup? If so, what happened?

19. What is the nicest thing a friend has ever done for you?

20. Do you agree or disagree with this statement? Friendship is important to me.

# CHAPTER 20: LOVE AND ROMANCE

Human beings have a long history of searching for love and romance. Love can help us form deep bonds, feel safe and connected and enhance our overall quality of life. Love and romance can also create deep wounds that we need to heal. Whether you are romantically partnered or not, I invite you to use these prompts to explore your thoughts as well as your current and past experiences with love and romance.

1. Describe your early role models for romantic relationships?

2. Who was your first crush?

3. Describe your feelings about your current romantic relationship or relationship status.

4. Finish this sentence: I feel most loved when...

5. Is intellectual stimulation important to you in a romantic relationship?

6. Is physical attraction important to you in a romantic relationship?

7. What is a dealbreaker for you in a romantic relationship?

8. What confuses you about love?

9.  Have you ever experienced love at first sight? If yes, discuss.

10. How have your beliefs about love and romance changed over time?

11. Have you ever loved and lost?

12. Do you believe in soul mates? Why or why not?

13. What makes you feel most desired?

14. What are your thoughts on monogamy?

15. Do you agree or disagree with this statement? Love is a choice.

16. What is your love language?

17. Do you consider yourself a jealous person? Why or why not?

18. Have you ever broken someone's heart?

19. Do you believe in second chances? Why or why not?

20. What do you believe is the foundation of a healthy romantic relationship?

# CHAPTER 21: SPIRITUALITY

Spirituality refers to our connection to something greater than ourselves. Something beyond our egos and our own suffering. Spirituality is how our spirit communicates. For some, spirituality is connected with religion or the worship of a high power. For others, spirituality may be found in things outside of religion such as nature, music, art, movement, philanthropy, mindfulness, etc. These prompts are designed to help you explore your unique relationship with spirituality and perhaps inspire new avenues of spiritual pursuit.

1. What does spirituality mean to you?

2. Finish this sentence: I have faith in...

3. What role did spirituality play in your childhood?

4. What role does spirituality currently play in your everyday life?

5. How satisfied are you with the time and space you create in your life for spirituality?

6. What spiritual avenues are you curious about exploring?

7. What support or guidance would be helpful for you in your spiritual growth?

8. What type of connection does your spirit long for?

9. Do you prefer solo or group spiritual pursuits?

10. Have you tried any spiritual paths in the past that you would like to revisit?

11. Do you believe in guardian angels? Why or why not?

12. Have you ever had what you consider to be a spiritual experience? Explain.

13. What questions about life would you like to have the answers to?

14. What do you think happens when we die?

15. When was the last time you experienced a sense of awe or wonder?

16. What environments give you a sense of spiritual connectedness?

17. Who were some of your greatest spiritual teachers?

18. Do you have a spiritual connection with music? Discuss.

19. How do you express your creativity?

20. What makes your spiritual journey unique?

# CHAPTER 22: AGING

Year after year, we all add digits to our chronological age. At a conceptual level, we understand that aging is a normal part of life, yet many of us still struggle to accept it. On the one hand, we know that with age comes wisdom and perhaps a sense of freedom, but on the other hand, we fear it, hide from it and try to stop it. I invite you to use these prompts to examine your own thoughts and feelings about the aging process.

1. How does it feel to be the age you are currently?

2. How has the aging process changed your physical body?

3. How has the aging process impacted your emotional health?

4. How have your hobbies and interests changed as you've aged?

5. How has aging been a gift to you?

6.  What scares you the most about aging?

7.  What could help make the aging process more manageable?

8.  What was your favorite age you've ever been and why?

9. Which age in your life would you consider the most difficult?

10. If you could go back in time and revisit a season of your life, which period would you revisit and why?

11. What time in your life was filled with the most change and growth?

12. What has remained consistent in your life over the years?

13. How have you changed the most over the years?

14. What does "aging gracefully" mean to you?

15. Who in your life could you consider to be an "aging role model"?

16. What do you want to believe about aging?

17. What advice would you give your younger self about making the aging process easier?

18. What are your thoughts on this statement: "Time has a way of showing us what really matters."

19. If you could stay the age you are now forever, but everyone around you continued to age, would you do it? Why or why not?

20. Imagine you are at your 100th birthday celebration, and you are to give a short speech about what mattered most to you in your life. What would you say?

# CHAPTER 23: PERSONAL GROWTH

Everything that is living is growing. Our beautiful brains, bodies and spirits are all designed for growth and evolution. Personal growth is the direct result of the choices we make each and every day. The choices in how we spend our time and use our words. Use these prompts to reflect on your own personal growth journey and inspire your future evolution.

1.  Describe three ways you have changed over the past year.

2.  What would you like to learn or try for the first time?

3. What would your 16-year-old self think about who you are now?

4. Who has been a great influence on your personal growth?

5. What has been your most impactful personal growth experience?

6. What family patterns have you broken with your own personal growth?

7. What hobbies or interests do you have that foster personal growth?

8. How do education and learning relate to your personal growth?

9.  What travel destinations are you curious about exploring?

10. What is a current life challenge that is inspiring you to grow?

11. How are you proactive about pursuing your personal growth?

12. What is your biggest obstacle to personal growth right now?

13. What daily activities take up most of your time? Do these activities contribute to or detract from your personal growth?

14. Do you consider yourself to be a curious person? Why or why not?

15. Describe a recent moment when you've been aware of your personal growth.

16. What would you like to be different about your life five years from now?

17. What self-care activities do you engage in that contribute to your well-being?

18. What is missing from your life right now that feels necessary for growth?

19. How do you help others on their personal growth journeys?

20. Is there something in your life that you need to let go of to move towards living the best version of your life?

# BONUS CHAPTER: MINDFULNESS

It is difficult to imagine living a true life in balance without mindfulness. In the simplest terms, mindfulness refers to being with ourselves in the present moment without judgment or attachment. Mindfulness is the truest expression of our mind, body and spirit without the distraction of harsh criticisms, expectations or obligations. Mindfulness means resisting our urge to label something as right or wrong/good or bad and instead seeing it for the truth and reality of what it is. Mindfulness is a way of life and a deep belief that we aren't defined by what we do but rather by who we are in each fleeting moment... subject to change and evolution.

1.  How do you practice mindfulness in your life?

2. Is being in the present moment difficult for you? Why or why not?

3. What distractions do you need to manage to improve your mindfulness?

4. What is your relationship with multi-tasking?

5. Do you feel like you always rush from one thing to the next? Discuss.

6. What is your ideal temperature for maximum comfort?

7. What everyday sounds make up the soundtrack to your life?

8. What is something you tend to do on autopilot? How could you make this particular task more mindful?

9. How does technology affect your mindfulness?

10. Who or what in your life deserves your full, undivided attention?

Made in United States
Troutdale, OR
11/04/2024

24425365R00108